IRAQ

IRAQ
OUTSIDE LOOKING IN
By William Paylor

IRAQ
Outside Looking In

Iraq Outside Looking

Iraq Outside Looking

As of June 24-05 nearly 2,000 Coalition Troops have been killed.

William Paylor

Of the Two Thousand Troops that have died, almost 1800 of them were Americans. I thought we had some friends fighting with us in this war?

The end is near

IRAQ

OUTSIDE LOOKING IN

Art Work By Nick Destefano

IRAQ

Outside Looking In

Wars have been fought centuries, and today we are still fighting. Many would say sometimes there is no other way. It seems to me that America always has to make the first stand. And each time our young men and women are the first to die. But why must we die for countries that hate us passionately? To die for your country is understandable. But to lay down your life for a country that hates you, is hard to live with.

William Paylor

I would like to dedicate this book of poems to all the soldiers that are fighting and those who have died in the Iraq and Afghan wars.

Many young men and women have died fighting for freedom in a country not their own. America always takes up the cause if it is in her best interest. And at the end of the day all you have left is shattered lives and lost of life.

Iraq Outside Looking In

1. The Fighting Rages On
2. How Many Of Us Must Die
3. Stopping This War
4. The Belly Of The Beast
5. One Step Forward Two Steps Back
6. The Sun Don't Shine Here Anymore
7. Rise
8. War
9. The Beginning
10. The Fight Must Go On
11. The Request
12. Crystal Clear
13. One By One
14. No One Lives Forever
15. Brings The Boys Home
16. If The Wind Blows
17. Battlefield
18. The Invisible Soldiers
19. A Hero
20. One Day Soon
21. I Remember
22. The Fight
23. The Other Side
24. Enemy I Cannot See
25. Freedom Fighter
26. A Time To Die
27. Casualties Of War
28. Today We Fight
29. A Thousand Dead And Counting
30. If I Were Truly Free
31. Come Walk With Me
32. Why Must I Fight
33. A Dream
34. Politics
35. What's The Difference
36. News Flash
37. Dying
38. More To Come
39. The Price

Outside Looking In

William Paylor

The Fighting Rages On

This war started out like a walk in the park

But then reality step in and it's been a living hell every since.

Death stalks every soldier each and every minute of the day.

A city is taken, and then retaken by the enemy.

How can we win this war?

The enemy has no fear, this is his home, he believes that he's right.

The fighting rages on

For centuries, in this part of the world the fighting has continued raging on

But now we believe we can stop it.

We can do what so many before have tried and failed.

The fighting rages on,

Others have been here before.

Let's hope the outcome is better this time around.

The fighting rages on....

IRAQ

How Many Of Us Must Die?

Who left us American's with the duty and responsibility to keep the world safe?

How many of us must die?

Why is it necessary for our brothers and sisters to be the first to go and defend?

How many of us must die?

When our soldiers are being killed and mutilated, do you see the rest of the world coming to our defense?

How many of us must die?

Our sons and daughters growing up calling their fathers and mothers heroes,

But it would be much better to have them home and safe.

How many of us must die?

William Paylor

Stopping this war is like holding water in your hand. Some of it is bound to slip thru your fingers.

IRAQ

Belly OF The Beast

Each day we fight the beast with all our might.

And each day the beast grows stronger.

The beast knows no fear.

The beast is never tired

You can never let your guard down

If you do death will follow quickly.

The beast is hungry

It won't listen, it can't hear, it only

Knows death and pain. The beast has a mind of it's own.

The beast has it's own agenda.

And peace is not on it

The belly of the beast is filled with hate and anger.

The beast only sees and hears what it wants to.

If you kill the beast another takes its place.

The belly of the beast

William Paylor

One Step Forward Two-Steps Back.

Progress is slow

Like progress, war is slow you make a push

Then you get pushed back.

You take control of a city then you lose it.

The death toll is high, but if you stop now all of your Comrades would have died for nothing.

So you push, take a step back and push again

And you keep pushing till the very end.

IRAQ

The Sun Don't Shine Here Any more

My heart is heavy, the lost of life is unreal
Each day another life falls by the waste side.
Why?
The answer is still unclear; they say it's about freedom
Some say it's about oil
What do I Know? In my heart it's clear, the innocent are dying everyday.
In my heart the sun don't shine any more.
And it won't shine till all the soldiers come home.

William Paylor

Rise

Rise my Muslim brothers and sisters
Rise
Don't let your leaders lead you to your graves
Rise
If you don't have drinking water
You must rise
If you don't have heath care
Rise
If your children don't have adequate schools
Rise
If your leaders have billions of dollars
And you are starving
Rise
Free yourself
Rise
Rise and see the world as it truly is
See the freedoms,
See the deceptions.
Try to solve the deceptions
Rise my brothers and sisters
Feel the freedom that awaits you
Rise my brothers and sisters

Don't teach your children how to die
Teach them how to live
Rise
See the light
Feel the freedom
Rise

William Paylor

War

Who wins in war?

Governments

Is war right, is it just?

For centuries men have fought wars

Is the right always right?

Or, is the most powerful always right?

War is part of us and will always be

For now and for many years to come,

William Paylor

The Beginning of the End

THE FIGHT MUST GO ON NO MATTER WHAT

William Paylor

The Request

The killing must stop, and then the living can began to live.
War is a tool of death and it will kill to the very end.
It's a widow maker and a heart breaker, a devastator of all.
The long journey for peace is endless. The road will be deadly and tireless,
Death is always around the bend lurking and waiting.
But the request was for peace, so we must move on to the very end.
And some how make the request a reality

William Paylor

Crystal Clear
Will there ever be peace?
No
Will we ever see peace in the Middle East?
No
Will total peace ever exist?
No
Will soldiers around the world stop fighting and say there's got to be a better way.
No
How can there be peace without trust?
It's crystal clear total peace will never exist

As long as man is greedy, deceptive, dishonest our problems will remain

It's all too crystal clear.

IRAQ

One by One
We won the battle, but the war goes on.

Each day a solider dies,

Some days two or three

In the midst of all of this are the people of Iraq.

Innocent families being torn apart, and the not so innocent.

The families back home wondering will their love one's make it back to them?

What was this war about again?

One by one they died...
One
By
One

William Paylor

No One Lives Forever

Into the valley we walk sometimes alone

Sometimes with a friend or loved one

But we walk, our path is uncertain, but we continue to travel.

We see unbelievable sights along the way,

We gaze in amazement but we must move on.

We do things that no one would ever believe. But our journey must go on.

The day turns to night and the night turns to day

Week's turn into months and months turns to years.
But still we must go on.

When we started the journey the roads were wide and long
But now the road starts to get narrow and small.

Now up ahead I can see the end of the journey,

That I started sometime ago is now coming to an end.
No one lives forever...

IRAQ

Bring The Boys Home
Another car bomb blows up

Bring the boys home

A man drives up to a checkpoint
His car explodes killing two soldiers
Bring the boys home

A hotel is attacked killing a diplomat

Bring the boys home

A young soldier is killed while giving food and water to the poor,

Bring the boys home
People who have never had freedom are now free.
Bring the boys home

A freedom for which young American, men and women have died.

Bring the boys home
Bring our boys and girls home

And never send them to fight in another Country's War,
Bring the boys home

Keep them home

Bring them home
BRING THEM HOME

William Paylor

If The Wind Blows

If the wind blows maybe I'll smell my mother's home cooking
If the wind blows
Maybe I'll catch the scent of my girl's perfume
If the wind blows
The dry desert heat will keep me awake while I am on guard duty
If the wind blows
Maybe I'll smell my enemy before he sees me
If the wind blows
One day this war will be over and I can go home
If the wind blows
Will this be the last time
That soldiers will have to died fighting in foreign land?
If the wind blows…

William Paylor

Battlefield

On the battlefield only pain and death lies,

There is no fun and games, just death

On this field only God knows the outcome

Oh man thinks he's the one in charge

.

But in the end
Only God can be in charged.

William Paylor

The Invisible Soldiers

Where are the invisible soldiers?
Who are the invisible?
The invisible soldiers are the forgotten ones.
The hero's that we don't talk about.
The men and women who will never be the same?
Sometime we walk past these heroes in the streets or see them in the malls.
And we don't ever recognize them, you see the invisible soldiers are the wounded soldiers that we never here about after the first day. They become invisible, they don't count
These men and women are causality of war. We seem to always forget about these soldiers.
These are the invisible soldiers, we don't talk about them, we don't know how many wound soldiers there are, and there is no special day for them. Some may never see again, or walk, some maybe traumatized and have mental issues.
These men and women are heroes too, but were are they now
Where are the Invisible Soldiers?

A Hero to some, But he was just my son

William Paylor

One day soon we will all be free

Outside looking

I Remember

I remember yesterday like it was today.

I remember then like it was now.

I remember the past and I see the future.

I remember the pain of times past

And the joy of now,

Yes, I remember now and then.

I remember the wars of yesterday

I remember...

IRAQ

The Fight

It was not my fight but I had no choice,
So I fought
I did not want to fight, but I was told to
So I fought
Sometimes they call us heroes.
Why?

Because we fight

We had no choice.

.

There was a fight.

And we fought to the end.

William Paylor

THE OTHER SIDE

They say it's their right
How they live and how they treat their women is their business
We say it's wrong, not fair, unjust, and inhuman
They call us devils; they say we are evil,
There has never been peace in this place.
And peace may never come.
To have peace there first must be knowledge.
A chance to see the other side to feel the freedom
But first you must want to see, feel, and enjoy all the freedom
Of the other side

William Paylor

Enemy I Cannot See

As I walk the streets I can feel eyes a glare
No smiles, but a look of why
Am I here?
No corners or ally's are safe
Every woman, man and child is no friend of mine.
The Enemy is here
I feel him I smell him
I can hear him
But my enemy I cannot see.

Freedom Fighter

Born in America land of the free

Home of the brave, then one day you find yourself in a jungle, or on a desert fighting for you life.

And the freedom for some foreign country, which you have never seen,

For a group of people that hate you, and everything you stand for. But you fight on why, it's the American way help those who cannot help themselves.

We fight on and we died bravely.

For America is the land of the free and we are the

Freedom Fighters.

William Paylor

A Time to die

It's never a good time to die.

When is it a good time to die?

On a Monday or a hot day

Or a cold rainy day

How about when the sand is burning hot, or when the sun is so hot that it's hard to breath.

How about just after mail call, and you just received a letter from your love one.

It's never a good time to die.

William Paylor

Casualties of War

War has no friends

Who are the real casualties? The teenager who leaves home to make money for

his or hers college tuition? Or the young lady, who hears the TV Ads,

Come see the world, be all you can be. Or the little baby that never get to see

His mother or father. How about the father that sees his only son sail out sea.

Never to return,

Casualties of war are many. Sometimes wars are necessary, but there are times
when wars have hidden agenda.

Then the Casualties of war would have died in vain.

William Paylor

TODAY WE FIGHT, TOMORROW WE DIE, AND THAT'S THE LIFE OF A SOLDIER.

William Paylor

A Thousand Dead And Counting

A Thousand dead and counting
I was told that the war was over.
But I see death all around.
A Thousand dead and counting.
Yesterday there were two-car bombing and many hurt.
A Thousand dead and counting
Kids in the streets playing like kids do.
A bomb on a bus explodes thirty five were killed
A Thousand dead and counting

Outside Looking In

IF I Were Truly Free

If I had a choice would I be here?

I don't think so

If my freedom were at stake, would I mind dying?

I don't think so

If the people that I bleed for would show some gratitude, would I fight harder?

I think I would.

If our leaders told me the truth would I mine dying for my country?

I think I would

If I were truly free, life would be simple.

William Paylor

Come walk with me

Come walk with me, and see all the pain that war can bring.

Walk with me and feel the heart ache that war leaves behind.

Come walk with me.

Walk with me see the devastation left by war.

Walk with me.

See and feel the hate and anger that war brings

Come walk with me

Endure the hardships of the families of war.

Come walk with me

War is a killer of all.

Come walk with me.

William Paylor

Why Must I Fight?

When there are problems in countries around world,

Why must I fight?

Why can't they fight their own battles?

Hell most of these people hate me.

Why must I fight?

Why is it necessary for me to give up my life to protect someone I don't even know?

Why must I fight?

Why should I leave my wife and family to fight a war across the sea?

When there is a war here that needs to be fought.

Why must I fight?

Why must I fight a war that will only benefit the politicians and big business?

Why must I fight?

Why?

Why?

William Paylor

**A dream can be rich and fulfilling, but living long enough to fulfill it.
Is priceless.**

William Paylor
Politics
One day you're the greatest leader in the world, you just bombed a country

That doesn't even have an air force. No loss of life

You have congress behind you; the public is supporting your every move

Then the war changes, soldiers are being killed left and right.

The public is pissed off, on top of that it's election year.

Congress turns its back on you, and all of a sudden you are the dumbest man

In the world, that is until the election is over.

You win,

Then you find out you weren't that bad after all

Nothing personal,

Just politics

What is the difference between a used car salesman and a politician?

None

They both are full of crap.

William Paylor

News Flash

U.S citizen taken hostage,

News flash

Six soldiers killed in roadside ambush.

News flash

Engineer shot down while helping restore power in Iraq.

News flash

More American taken prisoner, will be beheaded if demands are not met.

News Flash

Prisoners beheaded

News flash

President says we are winning the war.

News flash

One hundred and twenty soldiers killed in the month of June.

News flash

America has another Vietnam on her hands.

News flash

William Paylor

Dying is easy, now living that takes some work

Many more to come…

William Paylor

The Price

The price of war is death, hurt, and pain.

But wars still rages on.

How long? Forever and a day and maybe longer,

But the price of war goes far beyond the value of the dollar.

Many young men and women died an early death.

Innocent's bystanders are killed in wars.

Why?

In the wrong place,

At the wrong time,

That's the price you pay.

Imagine

Imagine driving down the street and a car bomb explodes, killing your wife and child.

Imagine

You are on your way to work one morning and four men force you off the road, then they kidnap you.

Imagine

You and your friends getting on the bus, a few minutes later a man stands up and says everyone's is going to die. Then a bomb explodes killing everyone.

Imagine

Every day and night gunfire, explosions, fires, bombs falling from the sky.

Imagine

Living like this,

Your kids living like this.

Imagine

William Paylor

One day some how it will all end

William Paylor

In time

In time any war will end, many will die. Some will even wonder why.

In time
we will forgive,

And broken lives will be mended back together and life will go on.

In time

The pain and Suffering will pass, life will move on.

In time

Our enemies will become our allies and friends.

In time

The world as we know it wont remain the same

In time

There will be change

In time

Life will have meaning,

Life will endure,

An some day life wont be taken for granted

In time

Life will be cheeriest to the fullest in time...

William Paylor

The Devil's backyard

Death and treachery is all around.
No where to turn, no where to hide
One minute you hear laughter the next gunfire.
The devil plays for keeps
This is his home
Each day someone dies.
Some are injured
Can the devil be defeated?
Should we be here?
This is his home, the Devil's backyard
The Devil play's for keeps.
He has no friend's only victims.
The Devil's yard is dangerous, filled with treachery and deceit.
Freedom is not on his agenda, peace not on his mind.
Hate, fear, death, is all he is about.
So here in the devil's backyard life is short
And death is only a breath away.

William Paylor

Face of war

The face is a young eighteen-year old just out high school dead nine months after graduation

The face of war.

A twenty-one year just married With a child on the way, Killed in battle, a son will never know his father.

The Face of War.

A pro football star puts his career on hold to serve his country. Killed by friendly fire a NFL career over.

The face of war

A mother's only son killed in action, what could you say to her, He died a hero

Will that make her sleep better at night?

The face of war

Played doctor as a child, dreamed of being one as an adult. Join the army to earn money for college.

Lost a leg and a arm during a Roadside bombing at a checkpoint.

The face of war

There are many more faces that we will never see,

Many homes and lives shattered.

William Paylor

IF God loves us equally, how does He choose who live and who dies?

William Paylor

What if

What if only the politicians were sent to fight our wars?

There would be a lot less fighting.

Forgive me, Please forgive me.

William Paylor

America Cries

A twenty- two-year old soldier was killed in Iraq.
His mother cried.
His wife cried.
His two-year-old daughter cried.
His two-month old son cried.
They will never know their father.
America cries.
A soldier loses both legs in Iraq.
He will have to learn how to walk again.
He will never run again.
He cried.
America cries.
One by one soldiers are being killed.
America cries.
A soldier's job should be to defend his or her country.
America cries.
But they are not defending their country.
They are defending a foreign country
America cries.
Bring our young men and women home.
America cries
If people want freedom in these foreign countries they must stand up and fight.
America cries
Bring our soldiers home
America cries
Freedom won't come easy but if they want freedom let them fight for it.
America cries.
Bring our soldiers home
America cries.

William Paylor

What is War?
Conflict, Combat, Confrontation, Warfare. Fighting, Hostilities Battle.

William Paylor

Rules of War
How do you fight a war with rules?
The enemy has no rules
The enemies don't follow the rules.
The enemy is cold and heartless, and life means nothing.
Killing is easy for him.
Dying for the enemy means nothing.
It's a way of life.
We have rules; the enemy makes up the rules as he goes.
To die for the enemy,
Is making a statement.
His rules are to kill as many as he can.
And Glory will follow
Following the rules of war is just another way to die
The rules of war should be surviving any way you can.

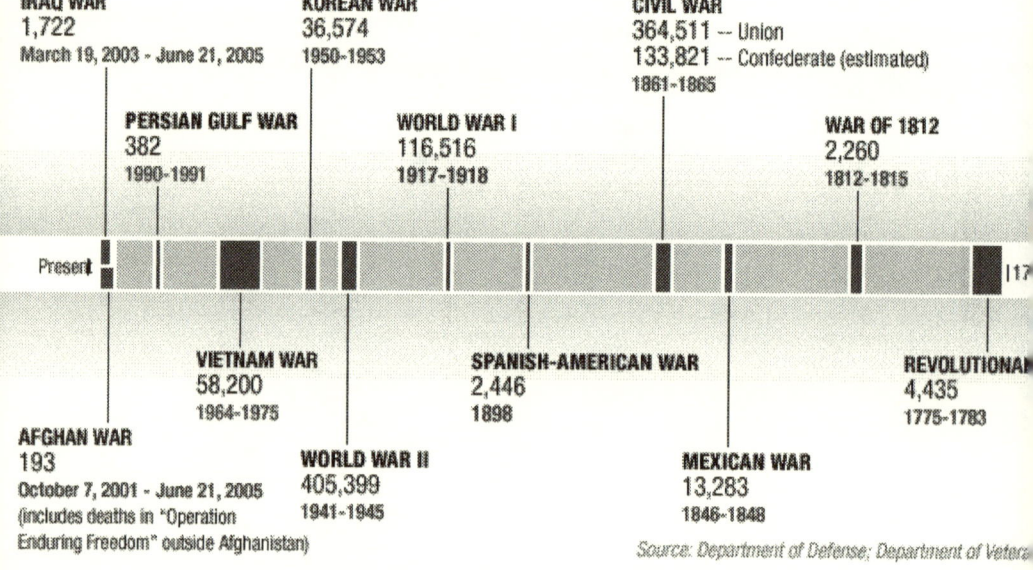

IRAQ WAR
1,722
March 19, 2003 - June 21, 2005

KOREAN WAR
36,574
1950-1953

CIVIL WAR
364,511 -- Union
133,821 -- Confederate (estimated)
1861-1865

PERSIAN GULF WAR
382
1990-1991

WORLD WAR I
116,516
1917-1918

WAR OF 1812
2,260
1812-1815

Present

VIETNAM WAR
58,200
1964-1975

SPANISH-AMERICAN WAR
2,446
1898

REVOLUTIONA
4,435
1775-1783

AFGHAN WAR
193
October 7, 2001 - June 21, 2005
(includes deaths in "Operation
Enduring Freedom" outside Afghanistan)

WORLD WAR II
405,399
1941-1945

MEXICAN WAR
13,283
1846-1848

Source: Department of Defense; Department of Vetera

Iraq Outside Looking In

Iraq Outside Looking In

ISBN 1411635655

$8.95

www.ingramcontent.com/pod-product-compliance
Lightning Source LLC
Chambersburg PA
CBHW020404290526
45785CB00005B/2439